the Choice

BY
NICOLE CARY

the Choice

Nicole Cary

Foreword by Scott Michael

Cover Design & Book Layout – Ernie Goyette

Published by Inspire Media, LLC
ISBN 0-9722332-1-0

Reprinted Meridien Marketing, RSA, 2003
Meridien Marketing
PO Box 13541, Mowbray, 7705, RSA
Tel: +27 21 425 0405

TABLE OF
CONTENTS

FOREWORD

When opportunity knocks on your door, you want to have the right key in your hand. Fortune magazine calls the new millennium the "Age of the Consumer." The rules of traditional business have changed creating tremendous opportunity, where vast fortunes will be made.

The book you now hold in your hands is a key to addressing how you as a consumer can capitalize on a new opportunity by becoming an independent business owner in a whole new industry. This industry, driven by the concept of "ProSumerism" – consumers profiting in business – has revolutionized our marketplace and is driving the "Age of the Consumer."

The Choice addresses key principles forming a foundation for success. It's about life and the choices you will make which will determine your future, stating the truth about success. I strongly recommend it to anyone who is seriously considering starting their own business. Prepare to be challenged, to be changed, and above all, to make "the choice." Read and enjoy!

Scott Michael
Independent Business Owner

FOREWORD

INTRODUCTION

Two roads diverged in a wood, and I –
I took the one less traveled by,
And that has made all the difference.
- Robert Frost

My earliest memories are filled with conversations about a word that forever changed the course of my life. It is a word whose explanation initially required long conversations on my mother's lap, and as time passed, she could simply say the word and I would understand the importance of the topic at hand. The word? **Crossroad.**

"You have reached one of life's crossroads, and you have a decision to make." It was a statement that I heard my Mom utter many times as I navigated the difficult process of growing up. Even when I was too young to understand the concept, my mother would patiently explain to me that life is like a road and as we travel down the road, we will discover unexpected curves and bends. Frequently we will find ourselves needing to pull over and ask for directions. Occasionally, we will find ourselves needing to make a U-Turn. And then rarely, she explained, we happen across a fork in the road – a Crossroad. The road is split into two divergent, radically different paths and we must choose which one we wish to take. **Contained within that choice lays the foundation for the rest of our lives.**

As a child, a Crossroad can be the choice of a friend – or the recognition of an enemy. As an adolescent, a Crossroad can be the decision to turn down a cigarette. As an adult, a Crossroad can be the choice of a spouse. Fundamentally, the choice of a path is similar to the touching of the first in a long string of dominoes. It sets into motion a series of consequences and experiences that await you along that particular path. It is the ultimate lesson in cause and effect. The trick is to anticipate what is inherent in the choice *prior* to making it.

What began as a simple explanation to a five year old evolved over time into one of those precious life lessons that a parent passes on to a child. It came to be known in our household as the "Crossroad Talk."

"Most people fail to consciously choose their paths because they fail to recognize a Crossroad when they reach it. Instead, they reach adulthood and find themselves in a life they didn't plan, as if they are simply along for the ride. They find themselves in a life that lacks purpose, lacks passion, lacks vision. **What they don't realize is that in failing to consciously choose a path, they still chose one. They chose the default path.** For some, they mindlessly follow the path of the person in front of them. Some choose the path that looks easiest at the time. Some treat their Crossroads like a coin toss and forge ahead without putting much thought into where they are going. But it is the rare few who treat life's Crossroads with the reverence that they deserve. They are the few who ask where each road will take them two, five, ten years from now. They are the few who recognize the power of their present choice as they stand staring down both paths. They are the few who live the happy and fulfilling life that you were intended to live. And so I say to you - **choose your path wisely.**"

As I grew older, I didn't need my Mother's presence in order to hear the Crossroad Talk. It had become permanently etched upon my brain. She had trained me to recognize a Crossroad when I arrived at one, and to preplay the consequences of my decision – to *preplay* by looking forward rather than *replay* by looking back. I have since heard it said that the price of discipline weighs ounces, but the price of regret weighs tons. I have come to intimately know the difference between the two. The power of disciplined thinking, of preplay, cannot be underestimated, and yet it is a lesson that today's society seems to have missed. It is up to you and me to teach it.

As time has passed, I recognize that so too has the baton of the Crossroad Talk. As a parent, a friend, a mentor and a student, it is a lesson on which I regularly rely. And so I say to you, as was first said to me so many years ago, **"You have reached one of life's Crossroads and you have a decision to make. Choose your path wisely."**

For those who choose the path of the many, theirs will be the path of familiarity. They will remain on the same course, reaping the same consequences. They will expect their results to change without changing their actions. It is the path which leads to a mediocre life.

But for those who choose to set their compass in a new direction, who will take the time to preplay the consequences of their decision, theirs will be a new path – a purpose driven path filled with adventure, excitement, fun and fulfillment. It is the path which leads to your **best life**.

I, too, stood at the same Crossroad that you now stand before. Two roads diverged before me and I, I took the one less traveled by, and that has made all the difference. **I hope you will choose to join me on the journey.**

CHAPTER ONE: THE CROSSROAD

"Today was once the future from which you expected so much in the past."

LESSON ONE: CHOOSE THE RIGHT PATH

The choice which lies before you is not about participating in a business venture. In fact, the choice which lies before you has absolutely nothing to do with the business that you are considering. The choice which lies before you depends only on whether you are currently living the life of which you've always dreamed. **Your best life**. If not, will you do what it takes to get it? Be warned that your best life will require of you a much higher price than that required of mere mediocrity. And therein lies the crux of the issue. The ultimate choice. **The Crossroad.** Mediocre or Marvelous. If you desire the latter, if you *choose* the latter, then congratulations. You have just stumbled across the business venture that can net you your **best life**.

When I first looked at the IBO marketing plan, I had just graduated from law school. I was buried under $140,000 of student loans and consumer debt. I was doing contract work – doing a little bit of work for a lot of different lawyers and charging each an hourly rate.

> **Definition Please!**
>
> *An "IBO" is an Independent Business Owner.*

You see, I knew from the start that I didn't want to sell my soul out to a big firm and embark on the partnership track. In fact, I knew that I didn't want to practice law at all. But I was stuck. I had made financial decisions. Horrible, awful decisions that haunted my sleep and discouraged me from answering the phone for fear that it would be yet another bill collector. I earned barely enough to keep the wolves at bay each month, never quite making ends meet and finding myself spiraling further and further into debt. With that came an enormous amount of stress.

Three short years earlier when I had entered law school, I had felt young and full of excitement. Now I felt old well beyond my years. I heard someone say that men die at the age of 25 and they are buried at the age of 65, and I was beginning to understand the meaning. I felt the light inside of me – the optimism of youth – beginning to dim.

Looking back, what I really felt were my dreams of freedom beginning to die a slow death. The gripping, miserable hand of my reality was extinguishing the sense of hope that got me through each day. **The present has a tendency to look permanent, particularly when it's as dismal as mine was then.** As I had mapped it out, it would take ten long years before I could reset to zero financially. Ten years of working a job and paying bills, just to return to where I'd been three years earlier. Daily, my mind screamed at me that there had to be another way, but the only thing I knew how to do was practice law. No one was banging on my door showing me an alternative. No one, that is, until I saw the IBO Marketing Plan.

THE SETTLED-FOR LIFE

I will never forget the day I looked at the business opportunity that you are now considering. I met with a local businessman on the UCLA campus. In fact, we sat at one of the very tables where I had spent countless hours studying during my undergraduate years at UCLA. Life is ironic like that. It was a beautiful, warm September evening and as he sketched out some numbers in the fading light, I remember thinking, **"This is it."** It wasn't that I saw the power of the Internet or the convenience of shopping from home. I didn't see the incentive trips or the tax advantages of business ownership. I didn't see any of that. Instead, **I saw a shot at a different future**. I saw a different path. In that moment, I knew that I was standing at a Crossroad.

That night on the UCLA campus, I walked into that meeting with the dream of freedom fresh in my heart. I was young and naïve and I didn't yet believe *the lie*. I was

> ### Definition Please!
>
> *"The Lie" is what we tell ourselves to rationalize why we settled.*

still painfully aware of this burning sense of *purpose* in my heart, this notion that I was put on this planet to do something *great*. I walked into that meeting with freedom as my battle cry.

It is not so with everyone. As I have developed my business, I have learned that few people are able to both cling to their dream of freedom, and live a daily life that seems to have no "out." The nourishment of their dream becomes too painful when the face of reality knocks on their door each morning. Instead, people stop feeding their dreams. They bury them. They settle.

Settling is a subtle thing. It is like a weed. If it is only trimmed from the top, it reproduces with amazing efficiency. Eventually, it becomes so familiar that it blocks our minds from remembering what we really wanted. Our mind is so powerful that when we tell other people "I'm doing okay," we actually start to believe **the lie**. We convince ourselves that leaving our families for eight hours each day is okay. We convince ourselves that making monthly payments for everything we own is okay. We convince ourselves that living a mediocre life is okay. And it's not.

The kicker is that we can't determine whether we have reached a Crossroad if we can't see how we've settled. Any settling must be rooted out and exposed. A formidable task. I've found that we must resuscitate those dreams of long ago before we can discover how we've settled.

Illustration: Have you ever bought a lottery ticket? If so, what happens the instant you lay your dollar down on the counter? We've all been there. We've all felt it. It's a moment, a very brief moment, between the time you pull that dollar out of your wallet and the time that you scratch off those numbers. In that moment, your childhood dreams are revived and you rediscover that precious commodity which has become so scarce: Hope. Hope drives us to part with *even a dollar* of our hard earned money. The hope of a different life, a better life. The hope of getting out of debt, of driving a different car, of moving to a better, safer neighborhood. The hope of raising your own kids rather than paying someone else to do it. The hope of pursuing your dreams. As we furiously scratch off those numbers, our hearts billow with hope.

And then it happens. The moment of truth. We discover we have not won. Though most of us logically know that we have a better chance of being struck by lightning *twice* than of winning the lottery *once*, we are still emotionally deflated. The sad thing about the lottery is that most people buy a moment of hope, but settle for a life of hopelessness. As quickly as they stuff their wallet back into their pocket, they stuff their dreams back into a box. They return to their settled-for lives.

But let's go back to that moment of hope that comes with playing the lottery or gambling or entering a sweepstakes. If we could press the pause button and camp out with the dreams that are in your heart *in that moment*, what would we see? **What do you dare to hope for** that you don't share with anyone else?

If you can *truthfully* answer those questions, if you can courageously examine your desires, then you have won half the battle in determining whether *you* have reached a Crossroad.

YOUR BEST LIFE

At this point, there are critical questions you must ask, but none have anything to do with the IBO Plan. You don't need to know how goods and services are shipped or how the money is made. All such questions are irrelevant until you've answered the only questions that matter.

These are questions you must ask not of a friend and not of the person who showed you the marketing plan. Instead, they are questions you must ask of yourself. More importantly, they are the questions you must answer. Honestly.

1. **Today, are you where you wanted to be five years ago?**

2. **If you do for the next five years what you've done for the last five years, will you be where you want to be?**

Stop. Think. Do yourself a favor and *don't* simply read those questions without processing them. If your life is worth living, it's worth planning. It's worth thinking about. So pause, take a moment and really *think* about your answers.

I know that I never anticipated being where I was when I graduated from law school. I thought the end of law school would mark the beginning of an exciting, fulfilling season in my life. Instead, I felt trapped and hopeless. Trapped because of debt, and hopeless because I knew that a career in law would never give me the freedom I was seeking. I certainly wasn't where I had planned to be five years earlier.

As for the future, I simply looked at friends who had been practicing law for five years. **The fruit wasn't on the tree.** Their salaries had increased, but so had their stress level and the number of hours they worked. They were as broke as I was, just at a higher level. I imagine it's no different in your job. Examine your manager's or your boss' life, and ask yourself: is that where I want to be in five years?

I knew that if I followed my current path, I would be no closer to my best life in five, ten or even fifteen years. There was a tremendous chasm between where I wanted to be and where I was going. It was my first introduction to "the gap."

GAP ANALYSIS

There are moments in your life when you hear something so profound, so revolutionary, you're quite certain you'll never again be the same. It is a **defining moment**.

Defining moments arrive wrapped in many packages, producing in us many different emotions. For instance, we Americans will never forget where we were and what we were doing when the horror of 9-11 first reached our ears. Fleeting though it was, it was a moment that forever changed our lives.

It might be something entirely different, such as the moment when your doctor confirms that you are in fact going to be a Mommy, or the moment when your husband proposes to you. Just a few short words, and yet you instantly know that your life will be forever changed.

I had such a moment when I heard a speaker explain "Gap Analysis." I vividly remember the crowded room in which I was sitting, the softness of the lights, the stillness of the audience. He had captivated us, and my life would be forever changed with just a few simple words.

As he explained, **Gap Analysis requires two things**. First, you must **determine where you want to be** – you must picture in your mind's eye the life you would have if time and money weren't an object. It's the getting honest that we talked about just a moment ago. **It's your best life**.

Then, you must **take inventory of your current reality**. For most of us, this is the settled-for life. He suggested grabbing a piece of paper and drawing a line down the middle. Label the left column "My Current Life," the right, "My Best Life." If you've been honest, then you will notice a gap between the two. **Welcome to Gap Analysis**.

My Current Life	My Best Life
Work 40 hour week for someone else.	Own my own business. I'm totally free!
Time with Family: Rush off to work in the morning. Spend two hours each evening with children.	_Time with Family:_ Work out with spouse in morning. Pick kids up from school and get ice cream together.
Marriage Building: One "recharge" weekend each year.	_Marriage Building:_ One weekend per month away together. Daily devotional together.
Car: Honda Accord.	_Car:_ Jaguar XK8.
Travel: Camping.	_Travel:_ ski in Colorado in the Winter; Bora Bora in the Summer; Italy in the Spring; Vermont in the Fall.
Charity: Sporadic giving.	_Charity:_ 50% of income to church.
Gifts: Only on holidays.	_Gifts:_ Buy my sister her dream car; send parents on a backwoods adventure through Alaska.
Helping Others: No.	_Helping Others:_ Help 100 families get free.

It was Gap Analysis that revealed to me how dramatically different my current reality was from my best life. I examined my piece of paper and for the first time *really saw* how much my life had drifted. Little in my current reality resembled my best life. I had reached a Crossroad.

If your current reality is radically different from your best life, then you too have reached a Crossroad. It is up to you to recognize it. Your best life isn't a fantasy, it's a choice, and the choice is yours. Are you willing to pay the price?

THE PRICE

We have all heard the old adage, "There is no such thing as a stupid question." That may be true, but there is certainly such a thing as a *wrong* question. Recently, I asked my eleven year old son, Mason, to do the dinner dishes. His response? "Why do *I* have to do the dishes?" **Wrong question!** I explained: that question stems from a selfish heart, and it reflects a poor work ethic. If his view of the world were one in which he was equally responsible for the work in our home, it would never have occurred to him to ask such a question. He would have simply done the dishes. But as he admitted, he didn't believe that he *should* be responsible for household duties such as dishes. And he has regretted that admission ever since!

My son was baffled by the notion that it was his *premise* which made the question wrong, not the question itself. Many would-be IBO's are similarly puzzled. They have been conditioned with "broke thinking," thus they ask questions like, "Do I want to do this business?," "Do I want to give up a Saturday to go to a seminar?," "Do I want to change my shopping habits?," "Do I want to listen to tapes and read?" They don't understand that NONE of those questions have a thing to do with the *real* decision that they face. The real decision is **"do I want a different future than what I'm currently doing will provide?"**

What makes these questions wrong? Simple. They speak to the wrong issue, for they are asking about the *price* that success requires of us. Hear this: **The life you want – your dream life – has a price attached to it.** It is safe to assume that the price you've paid to this point hasn't netted your dream life, or else you wouldn't be reading this book. Instead, the price you've paid thus far has yielded you the life you have. The price you've paid has produced the car you drive, the home you live in, the clothes you wear, the school your children attend, the amount of time you spend with your family, and the money you give to worthy causes.

I paid a big price to get my license to practice law. Law school was grueling and expensive, but that was the *price* for becoming a lawyer. It now allows me to do what relatively few people in this country are able to do – to stand before a judge and represent myself as an officer of the court.

My son Mason dreams of becoming a famous athlete. He sees the glory and the glamour and he's very talented; naturally, these are the things of which his dreams are made. But we live in a climate where the temperature regularly tops the 100 degree mark from June through October. Practices are demanding and exhausting, so the complaints are many. But that is the *price* he must pay. As I've heard it said, **he must do today what others won't so that he can have**

tomorrow what others can't.

If you choose to pursue your best life through the IBO opportunity, know that you will pay a price for your success. **Never negotiate that price.**

<u>Illustration:</u> I applied to law school to become a lawyer. Had I paid my tuition, purchased all of the books, but not attended any of the classes, what would that say about my choice to become a lawyer? In making the choice to skip classes, I would have been making another choice - the choice to flunk out of law school. Flunking out would have prevented me from becoming a lawyer. **Thus, ultimately, my choice to skip classes would have been the choice to *not* become a lawyer.**

The same is true as an IBO. My choice when I registered my business was to get out of debt. But had I registered my business, enrolled myself in the training program, but then not attended any seminars, what would that say about my choice to become debt free through my business? **Just like the choice to skip class, my choice to skip seminars – the choice to *negotiate the price of success*- is the choice to fail**

in my business. Thus, ultimately, my choice to skip seminars is the choice to *not* become debt free.

Remember, each choice you make sets into motion a series of consequences. It is the law of cause and effect. Again I say to you, never negotiate the price of success, for negotiation will prevent you from ever tasting the sweet fruit of success.

Instead, make the price a privilege. Take pride in the fact that you are not average. Take pride in the fact that you are willing to do what others won't, so tomorrow you can have what others can't. **Above all else, take pride in the fact that you've seen the Crossroad and that you have chosen to follow the path to your best life.**

CHAPTER TWO: THE VEHICLE

*"Go confidently in the direction
of your dreams. Live the life
you've imagined."*

- Henry David Thoreau

LESSON TWO: CHOOSE THE RIGHT QUADRANT

If you're willing to pay the price that your best life requires of you, then *make sure* that you choose the right vehicle to get you there. **Many a person has made the fatal mistake of choosing the right path, but the wrong vehicle**. They choose to paddle a canoe rather than build a steamship. Unlike a

Settled For Life   **Best Life**

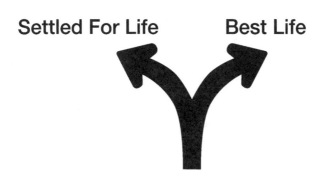

steamship, a canoe must be paddled to make it go. A canoe is fine for a weekend on the lake, but it certainly won't traverse the Atlantic Ocean!

How do you choose the right financial vehicle? You must first know what you are looking for – what features it must have. J. Paul Getty, at one time the wealthiest man in America, summed it up like this: **you must create a "golden flow."** In other words, your financial vehicle must generate money while you sleep.

<u>Illustration:</u> One of my business partners is a voice actor. He records movie trailers, commercials, and television programs. I assure you that even though you may not recognize his face, you have heard his voice! Here's what he does: He goes into a studio and records a commercial. It takes him a few hours to do that work. Each time that commercial airs, he gets paid. He may be golfing or taking a nap when the commercial airs, but he gets paid. Regardless of what he's doing when it airs, he gets paid! In other words,

> **Definition Please!**
>
> *Passive income is income that continues to come in whether you work or not.*

he creates *passive income* – a golden flow – a steamship. **He does the work once, and gets paid for it over and over again.**

We all have twenty-four hours in a day. Whether you use yours to create a golden flow is up to you. I would guess that Bill Gates uses his twenty-four slightly differently than the guy pumping gas on the corner. The difference? Bill Gates understands that from the neck up, we're worth billions, but from the neck down, we're worth minimum wage. **Never forget that if you want your best life, it's going to come from the neck up.**

Knowing that, and knowing that I had reached a Crossroad, here's what I asked myself: "what are my financial options and which of them will create a 'golden flow?'" The answer revealed itself in Robert Kiyosaki's book, *The Cashflow Quadrant*. If you haven't read Kiyosaki's books by now, I highly recommend them. His books will revolutionize your thinking. It's no mystery that all of them have been on *The Wall Street Journal's* best seller list at the same time.

The Cashflow Quadrant is about four kinds of income and the **emotional IQ** of those who live in each of four "Quadrants." As Kiyosaki explains it, the rules are different in each Quadrant and they each produce different results. However, the defining difference is this: the people on the left side of the Quadrant trade their time for money, while the people on the right side of the Quadrant create **passive income**. The people on the right side of the Quadrant are becoming **financially free.**

95%	5%
E Employee	**B** Business Owner
S Self-Employed	**I** Investor

TM

A WORD ON WEALTH

Since this section deals with how money is made, our focus is naturally on ... money! It is important to acknowledge that wealth alone won't give you your best life. Many a rich man is as unhappy as the next. As the old saying goes, "money doesn't buy happiness." But let's get real. Neither does poverty.

In fact, when I was penniless, I thought about money constantly. Not an hour went by where images of bills and late charges didn't dart across my mind. Down to the littlest decisions, my life was ruled by my lack of money.

I've heard it said that of all the pleasures wealth delivers, one of the greatest is its elimination of the petty problems in life. I agree.

Illustration: I love coffee. As far as I'm concerned, a day is not properly started without a hot cup of coffee. When I was practicing law in Los Angeles, my morning commute took nearly two hours and it simply could not be tolerated without a very large cup of java. Each morning I bought a bagel and a cup of coffee on my way to work. Now, this amounted to no more than $1.25 and is a purchase that should never have been a difficult one. Yet many mornings I found myself counting pennies, searching for coins that were stuck between the seats. I was broke.

One morning, my coin supply was exhausted. Not a penny between the seats, in the console, or under the floor mat. Even worse, every credit card I owned was maxed out - not even room for $1.25! Desperate, I paid for my precious coffee and bagel with a check - I was certain I'd be able to cover it. I was wrong! To my dismay, my check was returned for "insufficient funds." The bagel shop charged me $20, my bank charged me another $12, and by the time all was said and done, that cup of coffee and bagel cost me $33. And at that time in my life, $33 was like $3,000. The stress I experienced from that one event affected me for a solid week.

After years of painful growth and change, I have been rewarded financially and will never again struggle to pay for a cup of coffee. But through that pruning process, here's what I concluded: **Even though money isn't the most important thing in life, it affects the most important things in life**. It affects our stress level, which affects our relationships. It affects the kind of car we can afford, which affects our safety. It affects where we live, which affects our children.

Money also deeply affects our marriages. I am simply crazy about the man I married. I want to spend the bulk of my day with him and make the most of this next fifty plus years that we have together. I want to watch movies until midnight on a Tuesday and sleep in until 10:00 a.m. together without worrying about a job. I want to take a midweek jaunt to the coast or hop on a plane to Hawaii whenever the mood strikes us. When I worked a job, none of those was possible. Why not just quit? Because I, like you, needed the *money* that my job provided.

Like it or not, **our freedom is a function of money**. We work Saturdays and miss our kids' soccer games because we need the money. We put our kids in daycare and let someone else raise them because we need the money. We skimp on our tithe or throw away requests for charity because we need the money. Replace your income, and many of those problems are solved.

So yes, we're going to discuss money. In fact, we're going to discuss a lot of money. We're going to talk about making truckloads of green stuff that fill your bank accounts and free you from that debt laden, settled-for life. After all, **you are going to do the work of a millionaire whether you get paid like one or not.** Let's turn to the Quadrant and figure out how to get paid like one!

THE LEFT SIDE OF THE QUADRANT: "E" and "S"
(Employee & Self-Employed)

"Is the money you make worth the price that you pay?"- Graham Nash

There is an interesting phenomenon that governs money in North America. It's the 95/5 Rule. The rule states that 95% percent of people create an income on the left side of the Quadrant, *but*, the remaining 5%, who earn their income on the right side, control 95% of the money. Here's the good news: **You and I have the same shot at being on the right side of the Quadrant as did Bill Gates**. This is *Free Enterprise* and the beautiful thing about Free Enterprise is that *anyone* is free to join the 5 percenters. It is simply a choice.

Employee (E)

Briefly, I gave traditional employment a whirl. I quickly discovered that as an employee, my time belonged to someone else. I was an indentured servant for eight hours a day. And because it was a *job*, I didn't get paid what *I* was worth. I only got paid what the *job* was worth. A world renowned plastic surgeon who earns $10,000 per surgery will be reduced to minimum wage if he gets a job at McDonald's. And therein lies the inherent flaw with any job. You will eventually "top out."

Why, then, do so many people cling to the employee quadrant? Many people get trapped here because a job makes them feel **secure**. For a person in this quadrant, the security speaks to the emotion of fear. "Fear of what?," you ask. Fear of economic uncertainty. For most of us, we go to school, graduate, get a job and find that we have money to spend. As a young adult, we can afford an apartment, some furniture, and, of course, a new car! The bills come in. Spending habits form. And then we meet that special someone and get married. Now we really have it made because there are two incomes – we're rich! We buy a house and, with it, a mortgage payment. Of course, the new home must be beautifully furnished, so we take advantage of the many "no interest, no payments for one year" programs.

By their late twenties, most people find themselves deeply in debt, clinging to a job just to pay the bills. For them, security becomes more important than money, and they emotionally resign to the fact that this is simply what the rest of their life is going to look like. They settle for minimum monthly payments, car payments, and a big fat mortgage. They work hard for forty long years. When they retire, they must reduce their lifestyle, for their retirement funds can't support the life to which they have become accustomed. This is the typical story of the average employee in America. Clearly, employment is not the path to financial freedom.

Self-Employed (S)

As an employee, I recognized that it was not my boss' job to make me wealthy. It was his job to make sure I got my paycheck. It was my job to get financially free. Since I was looking to "do my own thing" and own my own time, I did what many employees do – I decided to "be my own boss." I moved into the "S" Quadrant by becoming a contract attorney and charging an hourly rate for my services. I was free to perform the work on my own schedule and loved my newfound sense of independence.

The independence found in the "S" Quadrant is very appealing to many professionals such as doctors, lawyers, consultants and realtors. Self-employment looks like the perfect solution for those seeking more independence, more recognition, and more money.

However, self-employment is also inherently flawed, as success here requires a tremendous amount of *time*. I found myself trading time for money again, when what I was searching for was a way to make more money by investing less time. I also found that I was working much harder as a self-employed person, because I was doing it all. **As Kiyosaki explains, the "S" Quadrant is the hardest quadrant there is, because if you are successful as an "S," you will work harder than if you were in any of the other quadrants.** As a self-employed person, you may gain independence, but not financial freedom – you'll still be paddling a canoe.

In fact, both of the financial options on the left side of the Quadrant are limited by *time*. The right side is not. Since **the vehicle to your best life must give you time back rather than take it away**, it is obvious that neither employment nor self-employment will get you there.

THE RIGHT SIDE OF THE QUADRANT "B" and "I"
(Business Owner & Investor)

"You are not merely here to make a living. You are here in order to enable the world to live more amply, with greater vision, with a finer spirit of hope and achievement. You are here to enrich the world, and you impoverish yourself if you forget the errand."

- Woodrow Wilson

If you're like me, traveling to the right side of the Quadrant will take more than just changing what you *do*. It will require changing how you *think*. Let's face it – I didn't pay $33 for a bagel and coffee because I was a financial genius. That moment was the culmination of the many poor financial decisions that I had made my entire adult life. In some ways, when I got the notice in the mail that the check had bounced, it was like a mini-Crossroad. I knew that **something had to change**. The truth is, I could have declared bankruptcy and erased the consumer debt. But something in my heart told me that the debt wasn't the problem. The debt was merely a reflection of something bigger – of a lack of self-discipline; of an inability to practice delayed gratification. I knew that if I didn't change the way I thought about money, then I'd keep repeating the same pattern of debt accrual until the lesson was learned. I heard someone say that **"until the pain of remaining the same is greater than the pain of change, you won't change."** I had finally reached the moment when I was ready to change. I was ready to create **wealth**.

I started to analyze the people around me – my parents, my boss, my siblings, my friends. I worked in one of the most affluent cities in the nation, a stone's throw away from Beverly Hills. I was surrounded by beautiful homes and incredible cars. I asked myself, "what do these people do? Who are these people?" I read about the wealthy.

Rockefeller, Carnegie, Getty, Gates. As I journeyed along on this quest for knowledge, this quest for **change**, something amazing happened. Wisdom began to whisper in my ear. Patterns began to surface. Principles were revealed.

I traded my beautiful, fully loaded mustang convertible in for a practical, boring commuter car. I tore up my credit cards and committed myself to a "cash only" policy. I budgeted. Most of all, I took seriously the transition from the left to the right side of the Quadrant. I relentlessly pursued the thought patterns of the wealthy. I retrained my mind to evaluate financial opportunity from the "B" Quadrant. It was in doing all of this that I found the IBO Marketing Plan – the vehicle to my best life.

Business Owner (B)

A true "B" business is defined by one thing: a **system**. Those who are true "B's" can leave their business for a year and return to find it more profitable and running better than when they left it. Unlike an "S" business owner, who in reality owns a job, a true "B" owns a **system**.

> ## Definition Please!
>
> *Wealth is measured in time, not dollars. Wealth is the number of days you can survive without physically working and still maintain your standard of living.*

What is the difference? "S" business owners are tied to their businesses. While they enjoy the tax benefits of operating their own business, they really meet the money and time criteria of the self-employed. For instance, a dentist is an "S" business owner. A dentist may own his own dental practice, his own business, but if he goes on vacation, so does his income. In order to make money, he must physically be there to perform.

Unlike an "S" business, in a "B" business, it's not the *time* that creates the money, it's the *system* that produces it. **A system is a proven pattern that can be duplicated by anyone.** Without question, the best example is the McDonalds franchise. Does McDonalds make the best hamburgers in the world? No. But does McDonalds have the best **system** for delivering hamburgers? Absolutely.

As Kiyosaki explains, from store to store, you will see the system is the same. Pay attention and you will see **pure duplication** - from the trucks that deliver the raw burger to the rancher that raised the beef to the TV ads with Ronald McDonald. Notice the training of young inexperienced people to say the same words, "Hello, welcome to McDonalds," as well as the décor of the franchise, the regional offices, the bakeries that bake the buns, and the millions of pounds of french fries that taste exactly the same all over the world. It is an **excellent business system**.

As a result, the owner of a McDonalds need not be present in order to make money. He can be vacationing in Europe or just taking a nap, but either way the system continues to generate money. True business ownership provides **passive income**.

Investor (I)

One other way to become wealthy is through investment. Again, you don't work for money - you let your money work for you. But as Kiyosaki explains, the key to being a good investor is to first be a good business owner. That's why he recommends that people who are moving from the left side to the right side of the Quadrant start as a "B," because true "I's" invest in successful "B's" with stable business systems. And, if you have a business that is up and running, you have the cash flow to support the ups and downs that come with being an "I."

*   *   *

After reviewing the four Quadrants, I knew where

I needed to be. Perhaps you now face the same realization as did I: I must get into the "B" Quadrant, and fast!

I've heard it said that when preparedness meets opportunity, GREAT things happen. I was prepared. Opportunity knocked, and I answered the door. Will you?

THE VEHICLE

CHAPTER THREE: THE OPPORTUNITY

*"What's my return on investment on e-commerce?
Are you crazy? This is Columbus in the New World.
What was his ROI?"*

-Andrew Grove, Intel Chairman

LESSON THREE: CHOOSE THE RIGHT BUSINESS

It is clear that true "B" business ownership will net us financial freedom. As we discussed earlier, money isn't the most important thing in life, but it does *affect* all of the most important things in life. If you choose to venture to the right side of the Quadrant, the only remaining question for you to answer is, what business?

> "If you want to get rich, just find someone making lots of money and do what he's doing."
>
> -J. Paul Getty

THE CONCEPT: PROSUMERISM

Billionaire J. Paul Getty once observed that, "If you want to get rich, just find someone making lots of money and do what he's doing." I, like you, found an entire community of people who are doing just that. And they are doing it with a movement that has revolutionized the marketplace: **ProSumerism**. ProSumerism is a megatrend that makes financial freedom not just possible, but possible for anyone who chooses to capitalize on it.

A ProSumer is a **profiting consumer in business**. It is someone who *produces* income as a byproduct of his consumption and the clients that he develops. Unlike a consumer, who simply spends money, a ProSumer is included in the profit loop.

Futurist Alvin Toffler first coined the word "prosumer" in his 1980 best seller, *The Third Wave*, in which he wrote, "We see a progressive blurring of the line that separates producer from consumer. We see the rising significance of the prosumer..."

How right he was! But Toffler wrote this in the same year that the first IBM personal computer appeared. There were no cell phones until 1984. The Internet did not become available to the general public until the first browser software came along in 1993. Indeed, the Internet did not enter the public consciousness until 1995 and did not become a vehicle for shopping until Amazon's virtual bookstore burst on the scene in 1996. In a sense, Toffler's prosumer theory did not become a credible fact until the Internet.

Why? Because ProSumerism doesn't fit conventional perspectives of how retail businesses are run. ProSumerism is about minimizing the number of points of contact between manufacturer and consumer. It is about linking the producer directly to the consumer in order to make an efficient transfer of goods.

While a single ProSumer doesn't possess much strength on his own, it is the banding together of Pro-Sumers – **the creation of profitable communities** – that drives our industry. In short, it allows every man and every woman to combine their buying power and take that bold, life-changing step from the left to the right side of the Quadrant.

THE ACTIVITIES: REGISTER, REDIRECT, REFER

Remember that a true "B" business is defined by one thing: it's system based. While the people on the left trade their time, people on the right duplicate their time. **As an IBO, we're talking about creating wealth through duplication.**

What do we duplicate? Three activities: **Register, Redirect, and Refer.**

1. Register: We hop online or call a 1-800 number and register our businesses for a nominal start-up cost. It's a simple choice – **either shop, or shop and get paid!**

2. Redirect: In the traditional business loop, we get in our cars and drive to a store where we make a purchase and take it home. The store is the middleman – they connect the manufacturer with the consumer. As

Bill Gates explains in his book *Business@theSpeedofThought*:

> *In pre-Internet days the only way consumers could get goods from most manufacturers was through tiers of distributors and resellers ... [today] the value of a 'pass-through' middleman is quickly falling to zero.*

As an IBO, we *ProSume* instead of *consume*. That is, we eliminate the middleman and handshake directly with the manufacturer. We redirect or reroute our purchases so that we now purchase everything we need to run our lives from our own business. **From peanut butter to toilet paper to contact lenses, we buy it all from our own business and have it delivered to our home at a competitive price.**

Why is this important? Paul Pilzer, a professor of economy at Harvard University, explains that upwards of 60% of the cost of a product is caught up in distribution – in the middleman. While your box of cereal may only cost the manufacturer 75 cents to make, you pay $3.75 for it because the middlemen pad their costs into it. When we eliminate the middleman, we create a pool of money that gets paid back to IBO's in the form of compounding commissions. The larger the pool, the bigger the commission checks!

3. Refer: In addition to eliminating the middleman, we have eliminated another staple of traditional business: advertising. Instead, we use word of mouth referral. Again, Gates:

> *Word of mouth is the most powerful means by which any product or company builds a reputation, and the Internet is a medium made for word of mouth.*

No billboard or TV commercial will ever wield the credibility of a single candid comment from a friend. Like referring a great movie or a wonderful restaurant, we refer a revolutionary business concept and get paid for doing so.

In other words, we are creating teams of independent business owners – **entrepreneurial communities that *connect* their buying power.** Herbert M. Baum, President of Campbell Soup Company, said of this century that:

Business will be reborn. It'll break out and people will begin to start little businesses that in turn will compete with the conglomerates, then become the new conglomerates. That'll be the cycle.

That is exactly what we are becoming.

COMMUNITY: THE SECRET INGREDIENT

While many Internet-based businesses are crumbling, this business' sales figures have skyrocketed. The difference? **Community**.

Michael Dell, owner of Dell Computers, explains that three things are required for success on the Internet: content, commerce and community. Content is the website. Commerce is the product. Community is the people. Dell says that most Internet-based businesses have achieved both content and commerce. But few have achieved community. **Dell says that the business that figures out Community will *rule* the Internet.**

Community is the high touch aspect of business. It's a handshake. A friendly face. Familiarity. Community is critical because it creates loyalty. As so many "dot.bombs" have discovered, online loyalty is a formidable challenge.

Illustration: Let's look at a typical online transaction. Barnes and Noble is an online bookseller that also has a chain of brick and mortar stores. Amazon.com is an online bookseller without any brick and mortar stores. Let's say you go online with B&N and find a book for $17.99. You cost compare at Amazon. Amazon's price is $14.99. Both sites have the same delivery charges. Who do you order from? Amazon, of course.

The next time you shop for a book, the price is the same at both B&N and Amazon. This time, B&N is offering "free shipping." Who do you order from? B&N, of course.

What's missing in these transactions? **Loyalty**. There's nothing keeping you in one online store or the other.

Nothing, that is, unless you are an IBO. **As an**

IBO, you have a vested interest in being loyal to your business. You get paid handsomely for redirecting your buying through your business and for referring others to do the same. In doing so, you give your Internet-based business a face, a handshake. When people have questions about the site, they are not faced with endless voicemail loops and impersonal emails. Instead, they have you, and you have your team. It's win-win. It's synergy. It's built-in community. It's beautiful!

THE DESIGN OF AN IDEAL BUSINESS

We've conquered the challenge of community. We've developed a duplicatable, proven pattern for success. What else accounts for the resounding success we've experienced? **We possess the design of an ideal business.**

In a recent survey, over half of North Americans polled said they would like to be in business for themselves if they could find the right business. But what is the right business – the "ideal" business?

Business analysts agree that there is a design to an ideal business – a set of standards against which you should measure any business you are considering. Here's the list:

1. Passive Income: You do the work once, and get paid for it over and over again.

2. Duplicatable System: A cookie-cutter business system that can be followed by anyone.

3. In Business For Yourself, But Not By Yourself: One of the biggest reasons people never get into the "B" Quadrant is because of their fear of the unknown. "What if it's too hard?" "What if I don't know how?" "What if it doesn't work?" Those little "what ifs" run around in our brains, causing doubt, because we don't have anyone to help us. We need a mentor, a counselor, someone to teach us and guide us to success.

4. Time Flexibility: You set your own hours and are not restricted by traditional business hours.

5. No Inventory: Inventory is for an "S" type business

that is focused on products. It requires huge capital outlay and places you in the role of middleman.

6. No Employees: Remember the "E" Quadrant? Employees mean human resources – benefits payments, employee assistance programs, salary negotiations. The costs are staggering!

7. Low Start Up Costs: Traditional franchises cost anywhere from $50,000 to over $1,000,000. The ideal business wouldn't be cost prohibitive to anyone.

8. No Special Education: The ideal business would have a self-contained training system that would enable anyone to learn the necessary skills for success.

9. Global Market: The Internet has made the world a much smaller place, connecting people across the globe. The ideal business would capitalize on this trend and allow business expansion throughout the world.

10. Inflation Resistant: In a down economy, people cut out "extras." The ideal business would be based on core consumables – "daily necessities" – so that regardless of the economy, people would still purchase them.

It is a list that I believed to be unattainable for any one business. I likened it to the "ideal world" or the "ideal marriage." Fictionalized versions of something we hoped for but could never attain.

My opinion has changed. **As an IBO, I now own a business that meets all ten criteria.** I know. You may be as skeptical as was I, and that's okay. But I caution you to be an honest skeptic. Get credible information and get honest. After doing so, **compare this business to the design of an ideal business, and you will find that they are one in the same.**

*   *   *

I will leave you with the challenge I gave myself, and it is all you need: make a conscious choice. **Make a conscious choice** to abandon mediocrity and embrace greatness. Make a conscious choice to take the path to your best life. Make a conscious choice to pay the price that success will demand of you. Make a conscious choice, and then, stay the course.

THE OPPORTUNITY

CHAPTER FOUR:
A FINAL WORD

"The life of every man is a diary in which he means to write one story, but writes another, and his humblest hour is when he compares the volume as it is with what he vowed to make it."

- J.M. Barrie

I look into the face of my newborn son and I see in him an unwritten story, an unlimited future. We jokingly refer to him as "The President," because in that statement there is this unspoken recognition that his future is unlimited. No doors have yet been shut. The truth is, I know he will do something extraordinary with his life, because he has two parents who believe in his dreams, whatever they may turn out to be.

It may seem a strange comparison to you, but it must be said. The person who shared this business concept with you sees the same thing when he looks into your eyes. Regardless of the past, regardless of your age or your debt or your schedule, there is a wide-open future that lies before you and somebody sees it for you. The question is, do you?

We've all been given 1440 minutes a day in this life. No more, no less. Whether we squander time or honor it is up to each of us. I challenge you to drink deeply from the cup. Remember, you have a choice to make and, good or bad, **you will be the servant of that choice.**

I will not pretend that the journey has been an easy one, nor that I have yet completed it. But the days of bounced checks, alarm clocks and stress are a distant memory. And when I look forward, I see my best life. I pray the same for you.

A   FINAL   WORD